O Come Let Us Adore Him

25 Days of Remembering Who He Was, What He Gave, and Why He Came

Felita Price

InSource Publishing

O Come Let Us Adore Him: 25 Days of Remembering Why Christ Came

© 2022 Felita Price

Published by InSource Publishing, Indianapolis, In.

To God, my Savior
who upended my life with His grace,
and anchors it with His love.

To my spouse. Thank you for the insights, the challenges, the jokes, and the backrubs! Your wisdom, erudition, humor, encouragement, and generosity have made this work deeper still.

Contents

Getting Started

Introduction

God walked among us. He was concealed in flesh, but His magnificence bled through, and human beings beheld His glory. I am awed by this. Jesus left the perfection of Heaven, the bosom of His Father, the place where He was correctly esteemed and appropriately adored to put on rotting flesh, take up a servant's task, be ridiculed, whipped, and die – so that we can live. What wondrous love is this, as the songwriter penned, that Mary's baby was the Word made flesh, the Son of God who came to rescue us when we were festering in sin. Astonishing but, oh, so beautiful – and sadly, as we celebrate this holy season, this beautiful selflessness is often lost in our interpretations, and our celebrations become as artificial as the tinsel on the tree.

My hope in writing this is that as we refocus upon the wonder of His coming. I hope that we remember the humiliation to which He willingly submitted in order to save us. I pray we will be transformed by the depth of His love and that we will be filled with joy! I also hope that we will be inspired to share this joy with the world so that they can, too, know this Wonderful Counselor, Mighty God, who gave up His privilege and came to save us from our sins and extend to us the right to become sons and daughters of Almighty God.

How To Use This Book

      This book contains 25 essays consisting of 18 Devotionals and 7 entries titled "Deeper Still." The purpose of the "Deeper Still" is to give more background while I hope still communicating the beauty of the events they address. All the essays are designed to be read one a day; however, they can be read any way you like. Feel free to skip around, or because each entry tells some aspect of His coming, read many chapters, (or the entire book) at once as you would any other non-fiction.

      My hope, Dear Reader, is that the devotional questions will cause you to think deeply about God, His character, His love, and what that means specifically for you, and for all of humanity this holy season and beyond.

Let this mind be in you
which was also in Christ Jesus,
who, being in the form of God,
did not consider it robbery to be equal with God,
but made Himself of no reputation,
taking the form of a bondservant,
and coming in the likeness of men.
And being found in appearance as a man,
He humbled Himself
and became obedient to the point of death,
even the death of the cross.
Therefore God also has highly exalted Him
and givein Him the name which is above every name,
that at the name of Jesus
every knee should bow,
of those in heaven,
and of those on earth,
and of those under the earth,
and that every tongue should confess
that Jesus Chist is Lord,
to the glory of God the Father.

Philippians 2:5-11

1

The Reason He Came

Stockings hang from the mantle. The tree in the corner, with lights twinkling, hosts gifts that spill beyond its skirt. With shouts of glee and giggles, children in onesies, with cocoa-stained lips, rip off the ornate paper that conceals the treasure. It's Christmas, and variations of this scene take place in millions of homes worldwide. Our gift-giving, light twinkling, star-atop-the-tree traditions, though touching, are poor attempts to elucidate the wonder of something often lost in the interpretation: the gift that God gave the world through the birth of the Savior.

> For unto us a Child is born,
> Unto us a Son is given;
> And the government will be upon His shoulder.
> And His name will be called
> Wonderful, Counselor, Mighty God,
> Everlasting Father, Prince of Peace (Isa. 9:6).

The child born, the One the virgin birthed, is the Son the Father gave. He has come not to berate us but to bear our burdens, not to punish us but to hoist our pain, our mistakes, our suffering upon His shoulders, to counsel us through our confusion, to empower us in our weaknesses, to care for us through our struggles, and to destroy the tyranny of sin that has governed us all our lives. It is the joy of His gracious mission that our celebrations are meant to portray.

However, as we prepare, it is easy to forget that beyond the mistletoe and garland, beyond the brightly colored bulbs and family gatherings, resides an event so incredible that the mind is lost – incapable of fully comprehending its depth, breadth, and mechanisms, but the soul is found, reborn in its power to save and to heal. What was that event? That God became one of us and lived here - and people, ordinary humanity, beheld His glory (Jn. 1:1,14).

How we celebrate this holy season can be heartwarming. I love a brightly lit house, Christmas fudge, fellowship with family and friends, and trying to convince my spouse to reveal what gift he has purchased for me, but Christmas is not really about cookies but about Christ; it is not about mistletoe but about the Messiah and the great length He traversed to save us - and the grace we have received as a result. Only obsessive love for you and me could have compelled Him.

This season let us remember that as a result of His communion with us, Christ has reopened the channel between God and man. By His sacrifice, He has exonerated us from the charge of treason against us and expunged our record of sins. Now, restored humanity, those who have believed, can enter His Kingdom, into His government of peace on earth and goodwill toward men. This essay's purpose is to consider why the Word became flesh and lived among us: to remember that when we could not go to God, God came to us. Let's open the gift of His Son and remember why He came.

O Come Let Us Adore Him

Father, help us to be mindful this season of Jesus' humiliation for it has elevated us to sons and daughters of Almighty God.

Meditation

"For God so loved the world, that he gave his only Son, that whoever believes in him should not perish but have eternal life." (Jn. 3:16).

Reflection

According to Isaiah 9:6 and John 3:16 why did Jesus come?

How does better comprehending the reason He came increase your understanding of God?

How does it increase your understanding of yourself/humanity?

How will you implement these truths into your life?

2

To Save His People From Their Sins

"And she will bring forth a Son, and you shall call His
name JESUS, for He will save His people from their sins"
(Mt. 1:21).

Angels from Heaven came to Mary, then to Joseph, then to
shepherds minding their business, watching their flock at night
(Lk. 1:26-27; Matt. 1:20; Lk. 2:8,9). Wise men, illuminated by a
star, traveled months to the place that housed Him. A duplicitous ruler sought to end
His earthly life before it barely began (Mt. 2:13). Happenings such as these could
only precede a seismic event, cosmic, really. What was it? God in human flesh - *like
us* - establishing His Kingdom of peace among the kingdoms of men so that we,
fallen humanity could become - *like Him*. The ancient church called this theosis.

> The Son of God came to us in human form to live the
> perfect life - that we could not live; to deliver us from
> the bondage of sin - that we could not break; to allow us
> entrance into the Kingdom of God - that we could not gain;
> and to give us life everlasting - that we could not obtain.

They called Him Yeshua. We translate it as Jesus; it means, "Yahweh
saves." Names were often given to indicate the will of God. Appropriate, because
Jesus came to save His people from their sins.

Jesus, Yeshua, when we couldn't get to God, God came down to us. Being both God and man, He became the bridge, stripped bare and laid down, so that we who were stranded might cross the sin-carved abyss and touch the face of the Father.

Jesus, Yeshua, that baby that Mary birthed, the One she held, the One who cooed in her arms, hid within His human fragility all the deity of God, (Col. 2:9) strengthening Him to live the life we could not, triumphing over the sin that alienated us from God's goodness.

Jesus, Yeshua, came to free us from sin's death grip. Not because we loved God, but because God so loved us that He sent His Son to be the propitiation for our sins (Rom. 3:25). Get this, the perfect, sinless Son of God gave His life for sinners. "For one will scarcely die for a righteous person - though perhaps for a good person one would dare even to die - but God shows his love for us in that while we were still sinners, Christ died for us" (Rom. 5:7,8). While we were sinners means that while we were *still sinning,* still rebelling, still estranged - Christ loved; Christ came; Christ died for us.

Jesus, Yeshua, accepted the death sentence for our sins. He stood in the place of the accused and now we who have received His resurrected life stand in His – the place of sons and daughters of God, joint-heirs with Jesus (Rom. 8:17). Adopted now into the Family Divine, God has upgraded our future – clearly, vastly. Now, instead of foreigners consigned to the outer courts, we are invited to come boldly to God's throne and call the Creator of the universe, "Abba", that intimate name that children called their daddies as they pulled upon their father's robes, then raised their tiny arms to be held, the name that flowed from the lips of Jesus, the only begotten Son, so close that He was in the bosom of the Father. Now we, sinful, broken, bumbling, mistake-prone humans, can say it too (Mk. 14:36; Rom. 8:15). We can breathe "Abba" through our tears when we are hurting and shout it when we are blessed, for we now have that same access; for we are heirs of God, and we have that same acceptance, for we are joint heirs with Jesus (Rom. 8:17). However, it is not on our own merit that we have been elevated, but because the only begotten Son of God came to share *His* status, *His* Sonship with us.

We can approach Almighty God because Jesus, Yeshua, "Yahweh saves," came to save us from our sins.

O Come Let Us Adore Him

Thank you, Jesus, for your descent to earth that allows us to ascend to Heaven. Thank you for saving us from our sins.

Meditation

For our sake he made him to be sin who knew no sin, so that in him we might become the righteousness of God (2 Cor. 5:21, ESV).

In him we have redemption through his blood, the forgiveness of our trespasses, according to the riches of his grace, (Eph. 1:7, ESV).

Reflection

How does His coming to save us from our sins increase your understanding of God?

How does it increase your understanding of yourself/humanity?

How will you implement these truths into your life?

3

Genealogy

The book of the genealogy of Jesus Christ, the Son of David, the Son of Abraham: Abraham begot Isaac, Isaac begot Jacob, and Jacob begot Judah and his brothers (Mt. 1:1,2).

And Jacob begot Joseph the husband of Mary, of whom was born Jesus who is called Christ (Mt. 1:16).

"You will find a Babe wrapped in swaddling cloths, lying in a manger" (Lk. 2:12b).

The Son of God was gift-wrapped for us. The One who would save us from sin's devastation was born of a virgin, wrapped in swaddling clothes, and laid in a manager.

But before the miraculous birth, before the tender swaddling, before the humble manger, before any of these extraordinary events that introduced the God kind into the family of mankind, there was a human genealogy - a record of births and deaths, of fathers and sons, of the begotten who became the begetters. A lineage of ordinary people, saints and sinners, commoners and kings, the hopeless and the hopeful, native sons and foreign-born. People like you and me. People who were full of greed, lust, and hatred - the same pettiness that hounds us today. Ordinary. Typical. Human.

Yet, from this hodgepodge of humanity, from this inglorious mass, God accomplished His most glorious work. God sent His Son through ordinary people, and from the ordinary came the extraordinary.

It is incomprehensible that God even desired to save us - given our treason. But to save us this way: this beautiful, unprecedented way that united God kind with humankind, consuming what was rotten in us and conferring upon us what is good in Him, so that we who began in ignominy could end in glory, we who began in sin could end in righteousness, we who began broken could end whole, we who began in death could end in life everlasting. Amazing.

So great is the Father's love that even in His holiness, He refuses to leave us in our wickedness. He would have been justified in leaving us hopeless and sin-stained, but because of His great love, He gives us not hell but Heaven, not the ordinary but the extraordinary, not the cheap gift but the most precious one - His Son.

God chose these ordinary humans so that we could receive an extraordinary Savior. Rejoice this season because He is still choosing ordinary people to do extraordinary things. So, no matter what you've done, nor how unworthy you believe yourself to be, God is still sending His Son, through the power of the Spirit, to be incarnate in us ordinary people so that the world can receive this extraordinary Savior.

So, the next time you want to catalog all your faults (as if He didn't know them already) and tell God why you can't answer when He calls, remember that God chose broken vessels to accomplish His most beautiful work. He still does. So, go. Tell it on the mountains.

O Come Let Us Adore Him

Thank you, Father, for choosing, loving, and using us ordinary people in your extraordinary work.

Meditation

And Jesus, walking by the Sea of Galilee, saw two brothers, Simon called Peter, and Andrew his brother, casting a net into the sea; for they were fishermen. Then He said to them, "Follow Me, and I will make you fishers of men." They immediately left *their* nets and followed Him (Mt. 4:18-20, ESV).

Reflection

God still chooses to work through human beings with all of our faults. How does this increase your understanding of God?

How does it increase your understanding of yourself/humanity?

How will you implement these truths into your life?

4

They

Behold, a virgin shall be with child, and shall bring forth
a son, and they shall call his name Immanuel, which being
interpreted is, God with us (Mt. 1:23).

An angel brought a message to Joseph in a dream. Gabriel, who
stands in the presence of the Almighty, came to Mary. Through
these angelic messages, God apprised both Mary and Joseph of
their calling to parent God's Son, the Savior of the world. God also instructed both
to name the babe Jesus, which means "Yahweh saves" (Mt. 1:21). But Matthew 1:23
above indicates that *"they" would call His name Immanuel, God with us. Who* would
rechristen Jesus, Immanuel? After receiving this remarkable assignment through
angelic visitations, I doubt that Mary or Joseph would defy God and name Jesus
differently.

So, who are "they" who rechristened Him Immanuel?

Perhaps it was the woman with the issue of blood, who defied societal
norms and pressed through the crowd to touch His hem and was healed in a moment
from that which humanity could not heal her in 12 years (Mk. 5:25-34). After
being healed through a touch of His astonishing power, maybe she is the "they"
who recognized that such grace belonged to God alone. Perhaps she called Him
Immanuel, God with us.

Or perhaps it was the leper, ostracized, hopeless, and untouchable until Jesus reached out and touched him, and his "flesh-falling-from-his-bones-misery" was healed, and the stigma of leprosy that clung to him like a stench was washed away (Mk. 1:40-42). When his flesh was restored like the nightmare of leprosy had never happened, and the weight of years of rejection, worry, and fear was lifted, maybe he recognized that such love and power belong to God alone. Perhaps he was the one who said yes, Immanuel, God with us.

Or perhaps it is us - all of us honored to know Him. We who have had our tears wiped away by His compassion, our hearts healed by His love, our insecurities removed by His acceptance. Those of us who have come to Him dirty and walked away clean: broken and left whole: with a "past" and walked away with a future. Those of us who have encountered the One who is full of grace and truth and have swapped our ugliness for His beauty, our pain for His joy, our fragility for His strength, then we knew, yes, God was with us.

We are "they" who called His name and were delivered, with whom He walked through the blackest night, for whom He died and forgave all our shortcomings and shameful tendencies. From these encounters that left us utterly altered, we recognize God is with us, and we are a part of "they" who call Him Immanuel.

Our lives, reborn, renewed, reformed, are the proof that God is with us. Immanuel.

O Come Let Us Adore Him

Thank you, Jesus. We have peace knowing that you are Immanuel, God with us, the One who promises never to leave and never to forsake us.

Meditation

Let your conduct *be* without covetousness; *be* content with such things as you have. For He Himself has said, "I will never leave you nor forsake you." So we may boldly say:

"The LORD *is* my helper;
I will not fear.
What can man do to me?" (Heb. 13:5-6, ESV).

Reflection

What does Jesus being, Immanuel, "God with Us," mean to you?

How does this increase your understanding of God?

How does it increase your understanding of yourself/humanity?

How might this enhance how you celebrate this Christmas season?

5

We Have Come to Worship Him

> Now after Jesus was born in Bethlehem of Judea in the days of Herod the king, behold, wise men from the East came to Jerusalem, saying, "Where is He who has been born King of the Jews? For we have seen His star in the East and have come to worship Him" (Mt. 2:1-2).

Wise men came from far away. They left the comforts of home and traversed through heat, sun, and wind, covering a distance that may have required up to two months. Exposed, they faced danger from bandits, demanding physical conditions, and difficult terrain. So, imagine this, harassed by the elements, weary physically, in danger from criminals – not for an hour, but for months. *And yet they came - to be in the presence of the King.*

How far will you go to be in His presence? Though the wise men were foreigners, they likely knew of the prophecy that a star would come out of Jacob and that a remarkable ruler would rise out of Israel (Nu. 24:17-19). The star alerted them to this move of God, and when God moves, light shines in dark places, planets form - miracles happen, and they were determined not to miss it.

The wise men were intentional. Even in our day of innovation, travel can be inconvenient; yet, devoid of our modern comforts, they still came. They prepared the beasts of burden, packed food and water, found and financed shelter, left their comfortable habitations, and struck out to meet the King. *The wise men sacrificed to be in His presence, and the degree of the wise men's sacrifice indicates the degree to which they valued the presence of the King.*

An invitation has been extended for you to come into the King's presence. Jesus says, "Come to Me, all *you* who labor and are heavy laden, and I will give you rest. Take My yoke upon you and learn from Me, for I am gentle and lowly in heart, and you will find rest for your souls. For My yoke *is* easy and My burden is light" (Mt. 11:28-30).

If you are burdened this season, weighed down with anxiety, grief, and fears – is it not worth it to take the journey, carve out time in your busy schedule as did the wise men to be in the presence of the King? Being in His presence gives us access to all that He is. In the presence of the Gentle Savior, the Humble King, the Mighty God, you can make an exchange - your burdens for His strength, your pain for His healing. What would you sacrifice to be in the presence of the King? Whatever it is, it won't compare to the glory of knowing Him.

The wise men came because the glow of a celestial phenomenon indicated His presence. So we also come to the light of His presence, and it is in His presence that we are changed, transformed like Moses, whose glowing face, after his encounter with God, reflected God's glory. Being in His presence means that we, too, will reflect His glory, and they will know that we have been with Jesus.

We are wise men when we seek His presence, not for demands but for devotion, not for wealth but for worship. So, this season remember, He came so that you and I, sinners and commoners, can come into the presence of the King.

O Come Let Us Adore Him

Thank you for the privilege of knowing You, and for being invited into the presence of the Almighty.

Meditation

You will show me the path of life;
In Your presence *is* fullness of joy;
At Your right hand *are* pleasures forevermore (Ps. 16:11).

Reflection

What will you do to be in His presence?

This season, remember how much God loves you.

Deeper Still

"the renewal of
creation has been wrought
by the self-same Word
Who made it in the
beginning. There is thus
no inconsistency between
creation and salvation
for the One Father has
employed the same Agent
for both works, effecting
the salvation of the
world through the same
Word Who made it in the
beginning."

-

**Athanasius, Bishop
of Alexandria,** *On the
Incarnation*

6

Wisemen "Magi"

Now after Jesus was born in Bethlehem of Judea in the days of Herod the king, behold, wise men from the East came to Jerusalem, saying, "Where is He who has been born King of the Jews? For we have seen His star in the East and have come to worship Him."

And when they had come into the house, they saw the young Child with Mary His mother, and fell down and worshiped Him. And when they had opened their treasures, they presented gifts to Him: gold, frankincense, and myrrh (Mt. 2:1-2, 11).

There is a prophecy in Numbers 24:17, "I see Him, but not now; I behold Him, but not near; a Star shall come out of Jacob; a Scepter shall rise out of Israel, and batter the brow of Moab, and destroy all the sons of tumult." Balaam, a non-Israelite prophet for hire spoke it after he was hired by Balaak, the King of Moab, to curse the nation of Israel. But Balaam could not curse what God had blessed.

The Wisemen (eastern astronomers who may have been Balaam's countrymen) when they observed such a brilliant heavenly sign, "His star in the

East", they recognized it as the fulfillment of Balaam's prophecy, uttered more than 1000 years before the birth of the Messiah. In the heavenly sign, the Wisemen recognized the advent of the Ruler, the One "whose goings forth are from of old, from everlasting" (Mic. 5:2b). So wisely, they came.

It is often presumed that there were three Wisemen (perhaps because of the three gifts, gold, frankincense, and myrrh); however, Scripture never gives the number nor the names of the magi. It is not vital that we know this, but since the names and numbers were left undefined, it leaves room for us in the entourage. Room for all of us, wise enough to recognize Him, to be a part of the group of wise people who seek Him, find Him, and worship Him still.

7

Rejoice with Exceeding Great Joy!

When they saw the star, they rejoiced with exceedingly
great joy (Mt. 2:10).

It was a sign, that glowing, celestial phenomenon that wise men could
not ignore. It indicated that God was up to something. God often allows
us to glimpse His plans through signs, symbols, and types.

Consider Abraham. He was 100 years old, and his barren wife, Sarah, was
90 and way past childbearing. Yet, when God promised to give Abraham a son from
Sarah's womb, Abraham believed. God counted Abraham's faith as righteousness.
Thus, being the first to believe, Abraham became the father of all who believe. At the
appointed time, God opened Sarah's womb - true to His word, and 90-year-old Sarah
gave birth to Isaac.

On Isaac lay all of Abraham's dynastic hopes. Born miraculously, it was
apparent that God had something monumental in store. However, before the boy
was fully grown and God had fulfilled whatever colossal plan God had, God asked
Abraham to give up his dream, surrender his hopes, and sacrifice his son.

Abraham believed God would raise Isaac from the dead. Still, what anguish
did Abraham suffer? But believing Abraham obeyed. He brought the wood and the
fire and took his son to Moriah to sacrifice. Abraham told his servants that he and the
boy were going to worship (sacrifice and obedience to God **is** worship). As he and

Isaac walked to the designated place, Isaac noted the wood and the fire, but not the sacrifice. Astutely, Isaac asked his father about the missing lamb. "God will provide for himself the lamb for a burnt offering, my son," said Abraham (Gn. 22:8, ESV). Abraham's response was prophetic.

Abraham laid Isaac, his promise, his son on the altar, and just as he raised his hands to do the unthinkable, God called to Abraham. Abraham raised his eyes and saw a ram in the bush. God *had* provided the sacrifice and *Isaac was saved!*

In that story, Abraham is a picture of Father God, Isaac is a type of Christ, and the entire story is a picture of salvation. It illuminates the reason the virgin conceived and brought forth a son. Abraham would not have to sacrifice his son, **because God would sacrifice His.** We should die for our own sins, each human for his own deeds, but God provided the Lamb in the nick of time, and rather than you and I bearing the punishment for our own sins, God's Son bore it for us. Jesus knew death so that we who believe could know life - **everlasting.** Abraham's words *were* prophetic. God absolutely provided the Lamb. What wondrous love is this!

"Behold! The Lamb of God who takes away the sin of the world!" (John 1:29). If we focus on Jesus and the love of God that compelled Him to save us this holy season, we will have reason to rejoice with exceeding great joy.

O Come Let Us Adore Him.

Thank you, Father, you have rescued us. You have provided the Lamb and we are saved; thus we rejoice with exceeding great joy!

Meditation

The next day he saw Jesus coming toward him, and said, "Behold, the Lamb of God, who takes away the sin of the world! (Jn 1:29, ESV).

Reflection

How does what God has done to save us increase your understanding of God?

How does it increase your understanding of yourself/humanity?

How will you implement these truths into your life?

8

The King He was

But you, Bethlehem, in the land of Judah,
Are not the least among the rulers of Judah;
For out of you shall come a Ruler
Who will shepherd My people Israel (Mt. 2:6).

The King of kings had come. The ultimate Ruler, as much superior to all other kings as the foe He conquered (sin) was more formidable than any other. The prophets prophesied of Him; the people anticipated Him, but when He came, many rejected Him (John 1:11). They expected a military leader who would expel the interlopers who ruled in their land, **but they misunderstood the problem. Thus, they disdained the solution and despised the Savior.**

Earthly rulers were not the true nemeses, so, the King of kings came not to settle a natural score but a spiritual one. The war was not with flesh and blood but "against the cosmic powers over this present darkness, against the spiritual forces of evil in the heavenly places" (Eph. 6:12, ESV). So, their King came not with military might destroying governments but with love and mercy for people caught in the snare of sin. Jesus came not with a physical sword but with a spiritual one, for He came not to pierce the enemy's body but to prick humanity's heart with the love of God and the message of His Kingdom.

Thus, King Jesus went about casting out demons, healing sick people, touching lepers, and eating with the swindling tax collectors and other sinners (Mk. 11:29). He spent time with children. He gave consequence to women, allowing them to sit at His feet and absorb the very words of God - learning. Even upon scandalous women, consumed *and* condemned – considered the rabble of society - He poured out God's grace, so much so that one of them, healed by God's love, washed His feet with her tears and dried them with her hair (Lk. 7:36-50). Jesus spent so much time with the forgotten, the broken, the guilty - the sinner - that the religious elite charged Him as guilty by association.

Not the King they expected, but oh, what a King He was. His reign would bring acceptance to the forgotten, hope to the forlorn, and freedom to the oppressed. He came so that those weary and weighed down with constant slights of indignity and pain could find peace, and those bound and ravaged by the power of sin could find liberty. He came so that those who were outside the gate, forgotten, rejected, could have a seat at the table of Almighty God.

This humble King, who though He was God, did not demand His prerogatives as God; instead, He laid aside His majesty and took the disguise of a slave (Philippians 2:6-7, TLB). He came to bring a different kingdom, a kingdom of righteousness, operating on the principles of God's lavish love that promises to transform sinners into sons and the broken into whole, and offering the Father's embrace to all who enter.

Not the King they expected but the King they needed. The King we all need. And oh, what a King He is.

O Come Let Us Adore Him

Thank you, Father, for sending the King of kings who came to administer justice, bring peace, and deliver us from the works of darkness. May we live to spread His Kingdom of love throughout the world.

Meditation

For He Himself is our peace, who has made both one, and has broken down the middle wall of separation (Eph. 2:14).

Reflection

How does Jesus, being a Ruler of peace, increase your understanding of God?

How does it increase your understanding of yourself/humanity?

How will you implement these truths into your life?

Share Christ with someone this season.

"...For our sake he was
crucified under Pontius
Pilate;
he suffered death and was
buried.
On the third day he rose
again
in accordance with the
Scriptures;
he ascended into heaven
and is seated at the right
hand of the Father.
He will come again in glory
to judge the living and the
dead,
and his kingdom will have
no end."
-
The Nicene Creed
A.D. 325

9

The Kingdom of God

> Another parable He put forth to them, saying: "The king-
> dom of heaven is like a mustard seed, which a man took
> and sowed in his field, which indeed is the least of all the
> seeds; but when it is grown it is greater than the herbs and
> becomes a tree, so that the birds of the air come and nest
> in its branches" (Mt. 13:31-32).

Jesus came to offer us citizenship into God's Kingdom. Citizenship is an issue of belonging; one belongs to the place where one is a citizen. For example, to be a citizen in the United States of America, one must renounce allegiance to other kingdoms and pledge to support and defend the Constitution and laws of the United States against enemies foreign and domestic. Citizens must also vow to fight against enemies, perform service to the United States when necessary, and take the obligations of citizenship freely. In return, citizens are offered the protection of the U.S. government.

It is similar with the Kingdom of God. Entrance into the Kingdom of God means that you belong. You belong to the King of kings. As citizens, we pledge our allegiance to God. We denounce the Kingdom of darkness, fight against its evil principles, and freely promise to live by the law of love that defines His Kingdom. In return, you are rewarded with His care and His protection.

How does one enter into God's Kingdom?

Citizenship in the United States comes predominately through *jus soli*, Latin for "right of soil" or being born there. Entrance into God's Kingdom comes exclusively through being born there. Jesus said that unless one is born again, "he cannot see the Kingdom of God" (Jn. 3:3). Being born again is a spiritual birth that happens when one believes in Jesus, "Yahweh saves." To enter God's Kingdom, you must "confess with your mouth the Lord Jesus and believe in your heart that God has raised Him from the dead…" (Rom. 10:9). This spiritual birth gives one metaphorically the "right of soil," or birthright citizenship. **If you have been born from above, you are now a citizen of the Kingdom of God.**

Where is the Kingdom of God?

Because the Kingdom of God means the "rule of God," God's Kingdom is not confined to an earthly territory; instead, His Kingdom can be found wherever people, by faith, have submitted to His rule. Jesus began His ministry by saying, "Repent and believe," because the Kingdom of God was at hand (Mk. 1:15), though no earthly kingdom was ever established. Jesus also told the Pharisees, who wanted to know when God's Kingdom would come, that the Kingdom of God was within (Lk. 17:20-21). The power and principles of the Kingdom of God are within those who believe enabling us to break free from sin and bondage, love, give, know joy, and have His peace.

God's Kingdom is now. We who are citizens can experience the benefits of belonging. When we are delivered from the power of sin, we have experienced the Kingdom of God. When He cast out the demons, Jesus said the Kingdom of God had come (Lk. 11:20). Whenever we taste miraculous healing, we experience the Kingdom of God. When we walk in His principles and reap the rewards of His wisdom, we experience the Kingdom of God.

God's Kingdom is now; however, it is also not yet. We experience aspects of the Kingdom of God now; however, the fullness of His Kingdom when, "He will wipe away every tear from their eyes, and death shall be no more, neither shall there be mourning, nor crying, nor pain anymore, for the former things have passed away" (Rev. 21:4, ESV) and all things are perfect for all time, awaits the consummation in the Age to Come.

Jesus came so that we might become citizens of God's Kingdom and experience the power and protection of The King.

10

The Common and the Miraculous

And she brought forth her firstborn Son, and wrapped
Him in swaddling cloths, and laid Him in a manger, because there was no room for them in the inn (Lk. 2:7).

God came to earth, and no accommodations were made. There was
no greeting committee, no pageantry, just a feeding trough in an
animal stall. Odoriferous. Incongruent. If a dignitary had arrived
unexpectantly, is there any doubt that the owners would have moved guests? Ruffled
feathers. Made. Room. However, because divinity was cloaked in humanity, they
only saw the outside. To them, this was just the carpenter's son. They saw the shell
and missed the Savior, the common, and missed the miraculous.

When God humbled Himself and took on the form of man, He refused His
right to be honored; He rejected pomp and circumstance; He chose an unknown
virgin from an insignificant place to be His vessel. He had no beauty that we should
desire him (Is. 53:2); therefore, when the King came, they didn't. They didn't want
Him because they didn't recognize who He was. They could have. Foreigners did.
(You know those wise men from afar?). **However, many who were near missed His
humble entrance and, as a result, they also missed His powerful exit - for they
are inextricably bound.** Consequently, when He shouldered all of humanity's sins
at Calvary, many judged Him a fraud and rejected salvation. They could not see the
Messiah for the manger; therefore, they missed the Christ on the cross. It was the

30

commonness that caused them to miss the miraculous.

The Son of God, the One Who is the exact representation of the Father, and the One who holds everything by His powerful Word (Hb. 1:3, NIV), walked away - for a moment - from His majesty and embraced the human experience from the bottom up. No throne, riches, or esteem - in solidarity with the least of these. Common. (Hmm, it is more apparent now why He chose the manger). He veiled His majesty, for He did not come so that we could marvel, but so that He could model for us how it looks to be a son or daughter of God, so captured by the Father, so transformed by the Spirit that as we walk, God's light shines in the darkness, as we live, God's love is shed abroad. As we work, they glorify our Father who is in Heaven.

So, this season, remember, when we couldn't get to God, God came to us. God came for you - no matter how insignificant you may feel. Furthermore, God doesn't prize social or economic status; it is not outward beauty that attracts Him, we don't need to be prominent to receive His grace. God came to fix broken things. He came to make beautiful what was ugly, to embrace those who were rejected, and to make sons and daughters of God out of sinners. Making what was common – miraculous.

O Come Let Us Adore Him

Thank You, Jesus, for Your sacrifice. Through Your humiliation, we have received the honor of being heirs of God, joint heirs with You, God's only begotten Son.

Meditation

Notice among yourselves, dear brothers, that few of you who follow Christ have big names or power or wealth. Instead, God has deliberately chosen to use ideas the world considers foolish and of little worth in order to shame those people considered by the world as wise and great (1 Cor. 1:26-27 TLB).

Reflection

That Jesus came to earth humbly with no earthly trappings tells us what about His mission?

What hope do you see in that God uses ordinary people to perform the miraculous?

How does this increase your understanding of God?

How does it increase your understanding of yourself/humanity?

"...We believe in one Lord,
Jesus Christ,
the only Son of God,
eternally begotten of the
Father,
God from God, Light from
Light,
true God from true God,
begotten, not made,
of one being with the
Father;
through him all things were
made.
For us and for our salvation
he came down from heaven:
was incarnate of the Holy
Spirit and the Virgin Mary,
and became truly human..."

-

The Nicene Creed
A.D. 325

11

"Away in a Feeding Trough"

(Hengel in Garland and Arnold).

And she brought forth her firstborn Son, and wrapped
Him in swaddling cloths, and laid Him in a manger, because there was no room for them in the inn (Lk. 2:7).

The word translated as "inn" was likely an already occupied guest room in a private home. Luke does not use the word for a public house where strangers stayed as he did in the Parable of the Good Samaritan (Lk. 10:34), but instead, he uses the same word that was used for the place where Jesus and His disciples ate the Last Supper, that word is translated "guest room." Such a home usually consisted of one or two rooms with the animals kept in the lower level at night (Garland and Arnold 2636). It is in the lower level with the animals where it is presumed that Mary and Joseph stayed and thus where the Son of God was born, swaddled, and laid in a manger (Green 129). But what was a manger really?

A manger was not a glorified, lovingly made crib. No, a manger was cruder. It was a feeding trough, the place where animals were fed. So our Savior, God incarnate, the King of kings and the Lord of lords, the One through whom all things were made - **He who sat on the throne, slept where animals were fed.**

God is the master designer; therefore, **Jesus came to the earth in this manner deliberately, to be approachable, to signal to all who are weary and heavy-laden that He would be the King who understands, the King who offers rest for us all.**

"No one sings 'Away in a feeding trough,' which is just the point. The Savior who dies on a shameful cross was placed in a lowly trough for barn animals when he was born..." (Hengel in Garland and Arnold).

12

The LORD is with You

Now in the sixth month the angel Gabriel was sent
by God to a city of Galilee named Nazareth, to a
virgin betrothed to a man whose name was Joseph, of
the house of David. The virgin's name was Mary. And
having come in, the angel said to her, "Rejoice, highly
favored one, the Lord is with you; blessed are you among
women!" (Lk. 1:26-28)

Imagine this, a potter at the wheel taking a hard lump of clay and gently smoothing it and skillfully shaping it into more than it ever could have been without Him - a vessel capable now of doing what it could not do before. Perhaps he shaped the long, graceful neck of a water pot pouring out its holdings, or a sturdy open-mouth vessel stuffed with earth, planted with seed, capable now of facilitating that which lives and grows – in both scenarios making the clay useful, beautiful, graceful.

This is what God did for Mary. The angel called Mary "highly favored". Here, Gabriel uses the passive voice, meaning that God did it. God was the One who acted; Mary was the recipient of His actions. God favored Mary by gracing her with His ability to accomplish more than she ever could have on her own. God does this to us when we are in His presence, and we allow Him to work. It doesn't matter how we looked when we came to Him, mean, selfish, hateful, or possessing any number of undesirable traits. Ever the potter with hard clay, God lovingly shapes us into vessels capable of doing what we could not do before. He makes us capable of blessing and not cursing, of spreading love and not hate. By His grace, he makes us *capable of showing others how it looks to have God as our King* – making us useful, beautiful, and graceful.

Mary was highly favored because God favored her with His grace. God gave Mary the capacity to be more than she ever could be and accomplish more than she could conceive. Because the Lord is also with us, the Omnipotent One is on our side, He can make us graceful as well. He can turn our bitter into sweet, our pain into purpose, our misery into mission, and our ugly into beauty, making us bless and not curse, build and not tear down, love and not hate - making us useful, beautiful, graceful.

"But we all, with unveiled face, beholding as in a mirror the glory of the Lord, are being transformed into the same image from glory to glory, just as by the Spirit of the Lord" (2 Cor. 3:18). Jesus came not only to save us from a sin-filled life of separation from the Father, but also to restore God's beautiful image within us. Let the grace of God shape you like the potter at the wheel. Allow Him to mold you until it is His image that others see: then, go light up the world with His love, His joy, and His grace.

O Come Let Us Adore Him

Thank you, Lord, for transforming us, for shaping and molding us until we look like You.

Meditation

For we are His workmanship, created in Christ Jesus for good works, which God prepared beforehand that we should walk in them (Eph. 2:10).

Reflection

What does it mean to you that we are His workmanship?

.

13

He Shall Be Great

> And behold, you will conceive in your womb and bring
> forth a Son, and shall call His name Jesus. He will be
> great, and will be called the Son of the Highest; and the
> Lord God will give Him the throne of His father Da-
> vid. And He will reign over the house of Jacob forever,
> and of His kingdom there will be no end (Lk. 1:31-33).

He will be great. He was born in a manger to a family of little consequence. The religious establishment rejected His ministry. He had no military power, no weapons, just a band of 12 unlearned men. He held no political power, no earthly kingdoms to rule, and at the end of His life, they crucified Him between two criminals (Matthew 27:38). Yet, the angel prophesied that He would be great.

We often call things great that are imbued with earthly power, authority, or strength. We use it for military leaders, like Alexander the Great, for his military prowess, and for rulers, like Catherine the Great, for the expansion of her empire. But at first glance, none of these accomplishments would seem to apply to Jesus, and yet, they most assuredly do. In the spiritual battle for our souls, Jesus has ripped away the barrier that separated man from God, snatched humanity from the clutches of sin and death, and delivered all those who believe into God's Kingdom of life and love. For greatness in God's economy is not power unfettered (that's domination); instead, greatness, in God's Kingdom, is power tempered by love.

Let me show you power tempered by love. As the Son of the Highest, as

God hidden in human form, Jesus possessed the power to cast out demons with a word, the authority to command the angels of Heaven who would have flown like lightning to obey (Matthew 8:16). Yet because He had come to serve rather than to be served, He used His power to heal and not to hurt, to give and not to take, to save sinners and not to save Himself. Through Him was it all created, and by His powerful word is it all *still* sustained (Heb. 1:3); *yet* **He suffered insult rather than inflict injury.** When they spat on the Savior on His way to die for us, He could have reigned down fire from Heaven. When they pulled out His beard and beat the Son of God with a cat of nine tails, He could have opened the earth and swallowed them whole, but He spoke not a word. When they crucified the Creator, He could have come down from the cross - easily. However, the Lord of glory, the Lord strong and mighty, remained - nailed by His love for you and me and His devotion to the Father (Heb. 12:2).

The Son of the Highest employed His power not for Himself, but for others, for you and me, to save us from death, the penalty of sin. For He made Him who knew no sin to be sin so that we who are born in iniquity could become the righteousness of God in Him (2 Cor. 5:21).

Now *that* is great.

O come Let Us Adore Him

Thank you, Father, for Jesus who, though He was in the form of God, He laid aside His power and glory to show us how to love.

Meditation

"Then a dispute arose among them as to which of them would be greatest. And Jesus, perceiving the thought of their heart, took a little child and set him by Him, and said to them, "Whoever receives this little child in My name receives Me; and whoever receives Me receives Him who sent Me. For he who is least among you all will be great" (Lk. 9:46-48).

Now there was also a dispute among them, as to which of them should be considered the greatest. And He said to them, "The kings of the Gentiles exercise lordship over them, and those who exercise authority over them are called 'benefactors.' But not so *among* you; on the contrary, he who is greatest among you, let him be as the younger, and he who governs as he who serves. For who *is* greater, he who sits at the table, or he who serves? *Is* it not he who sits at the table? Yet I am among you as the One who serves" (Lk. 22:24-27).

Reflection

How does Jesus define greatness?

How does Jesus' concept of greatness differ from the disciples?

How can Jesus' definition of greatness shape your actions this holy season?

14

Overshadow You

Then said Mary unto the angel, How shall this be, seeing
I know not a man? And the angel answered and said unto
her, The Holy Ghost shall come upon thee, and the power
of the Highest shall overshadow thee: therefore also that
holy thing which shall be born of thee shall be called the
Son of God (Lk. 1:34-35).

It weighs 13 thousand, 170 *billion trillion pounds!* This beautiful blue
rock that we call earth, is held in place by its attraction to the sun, which
it orbits from 93 million miles away, one complete orbit every 365.256
days. If the earth revolved too quickly, too slowly, or if it stilled, life would cease.
Yet it orbits at the right speed, at that proper distance, and we breathe - and we rise
each morning to the sun's rays and retreat each evening to its reflection.

But before this awe-inspiring precision, this pinpoint accuracy, the earth
was formless and void, and over the face of the deep, the Spirit of God hovered
(Gen. 1:2). God's power - hovering, *overshadowing* the emptiness, ready to move,
ready to create from the nothingness something astonishing as the Word of God
commanded.

God called Mary to do this humanly impossible, utterly extraordinary thing
- a virgin bearing the Son of God, and understandably Mary wondered how she could
accomplish it. God answered definitively: He would do it. His creative, powerful
Spirit would overshadow her. Don't we often wonder how we can do what God asks?

It can seem impossible to love when we want to hate, to work with Him in the saving of souls, setting the captives free, putting the broken back together again, or just at times getting up to face another day. We can't do it. It's beyond us. And so, like Mary, we ask, "How can I do this?" (How can it be?) "I am ill-equipped." (Seeing I know not a man?). Thousands of years and many untold questions later, the answer is still the same: God must do it through us. The Holy Spirit must come upon us, and the power of the Highest must overshadow us.

Overshadow means to appear more prominent than something else. Eclipse is a synonym. During an eclipse, one object takes a prominent position in front of another. Just so, the Holy Spirit moved, and His power eclipsed Mary's. *His* ability took the prominent position over Mary's inabilities so that God accomplished through Mary what she could not achieve on her own.

The Holy Spirit is still moving, still overshadowing, and still empowering us to move, live, and act like God. He wants to empower us to saturate the world with hope and love. If we yield to the Spirit, His fruit of love, joy, and peace will be what the world sees, and His power what it feels when we touch them.

Jesus came so that the Holy Spirit could overshadow us, and we could live through His power, and so that we, too, can have a part in bringing Jesus to the world. So, this season, seek Him, let the Most High's power overshadow you, then flood the world with Jesus.

O Come Let Us Adore Him

Come, Holy Spirit, breathe upon us and be more prominent in our lives. Overshadow our weaknesses so that Christ can be formed in us.

Meditation

But we all, with unveiled face, beholding as in a mirror the glory of the Lord, are being transformed into the same image from glory to glory, just as by the Spirit of the Lord (2 Cor. 3:18).

Reflection

But when the Holy Spirit controls our lives he will produce this kind of fruit in us: love, joy, peace, patience, kindness, goodness, faithfulness, gentleness and self-control; and here there is no conflict with Jewish laws (Gal. 5:22-23 TLB).

In what situations in your life currently, do you need God's Spirit to be more prominent? Be specific.

15

Be it unto me according to Your Word

> And behold, you will conceive in your womb and bring
> forth a Son, and shall call His name Jesus. He will be
> great, and will be called the Son of the Highest; and the
> Lord God will give Him the throne of His father Da-
> vid. And Mary said, Behold the handmaid of the Lord; be
> it unto me according to thy word (Lk. 1:31, 32,38).

It could have been scandalous - and deadly. A pregnant, engaged woman would have been presumed a fornicator. Fornication was punishable by death - stoning before the congregation to keep sin from spreading its devastation throughout the community. And yet, despite the risks, Mary's response to God was, "Behold the handmaid of the Lord; be it unto me according to thy word." Notice, Scripture does not record God telling Mary that He would handle her fiancé, Joseph, whose reaction could have triggered scandal and death; she just trusted. Instead, God called Mary to this complicated, potentially dangerous, potentially scandalous, but undoubtedly exquisite task, and her response, and I paraphrase, "I am your servant. I submit to Your Word."

How could Mary be so poised? Simple, Mary knew God's character. She knew God as the loving Shepherd who gathers His lambs in His arms and carries them close to His heart (Is. 40:11, NIV). So, she knew she was safe in His hands. She also knew God's power. She knew Him as the One who gathers the wind in His fists and wraps the water in His garments (Pro. 30:4). So, she knew she was safe in

His hands. She also knew the efficacy of His Word. She knew that the same One who spoke in the beginning and the earth formed and light shined where there once was darkness was the One who spoke to her, and His words are pure, uncontaminated, unadulterated, and undefiled -perfect, thus - powerful. She knew she was safe in His hands.

Is God asking you to do something difficult? Maybe to let go of something that is hindering you? Or perhaps He is asking you to forgive someone so that the person can see His power in You? And you wonder how you can? How can you do it? Be it unto me according to Your Word; Mary's response was exemplary. Don't you want to respond like Mary? I do. I want to hear God's Word and believe I can do whatever He asks. We can have this faith when we remember that His Word will not return empty, for the same One who spoke the world into existence and brought about this incredible Incarnation speaks to us still.

God's Word is effective; if He said it, it will be done (Ps. 33:9). So, when God speaks, we must be like Mary and look not upon our impotence but upon His power and despite the obstacles, despite the danger, despite the sacrifice, say, "Behold the handmaid of the Lord; be it unto me according to your Word."

Mary cooperated with God. She believed and obeyed, and the Word became flesh. This holy season, remember the wonder of God's Word, remember its power to create ex nihilo (out of nothing), and manifest into your life the healing, joy, and power that you need. So, cooperate with God. As the Word was made flesh through Mary, He came so that the Word could also be made flesh in you and me. So that we could manifest the love of God and others can know the Wonderful Savior and receive the gift of His salvation this Christmas season.

O Come Let Us Adore Him

Father, thank You for Your Word. Let it shape me into who You say I am.

Meditation

"For as the rain and the snow come down from heaven
    and do not return there but water the earth,
making it bring forth and sprout,
    giving seed to the sower and bread to the eater,
[11] so shall my word be that goes out from my mouth;
    it shall not return to me empty,
but it shall accomplish that which I purpose,
    and shall succeed in the thing for which I sent it (Is. 55:10, 11 ESV).

Reflection

Mary trusted in God's word, (Be it unto me according to your word). Is. 55 tells us that His word will not return empty and that it will accomplish what God intends.

How does this increase your understanding of God?

In what situations can you apply this truth to bring peace and give you courage this season?

16

Near and Far

> Now there were in the same country shepherds liv-
> ing out in the fields, keeping watch over their flock by
> night. And behold, an angel of the Lord stood before
> them, and the glory of the Lord shone around them, and
> they were greatly afraid. Then the angel said to them, "Do
> not be afraid, for behold, I bring you good tidings of great
> joy which will be to all people. For there is born to you
> this day in the city of David a Savior, who is Christ the
> Lord (Lk. 2:8-11).

Shepherds were notified of the Savior's birth, and so were the wise men (though indirectly). Outside of Mary and Joseph, these two groups were the only ones we know who shared this honor; yet the two groups were very different. The wise men were educated and probably wealthy. The shepherds were not. Shepherding was a lowly occupation. Often, hirelings, the enslaved, women, and even younger sons, those deemed lesser, were made shepherds. Yet, despite the disparities, both groups were drawn by God - for *the good tidings of great joy would be for all people.*

Jesus came to seek and to save the lost, and though He came first to his own, God extended the power to become His to all who received Him. God does not value humanity based on wealth, status, beauty, or ethnicity: none of those aspects which we used to categorize, then divide, demean, and destroy. He wants all. He created all in His image. He breathed the same breath of life into all. Thus, Jesus came for those near and far, for the lowly just the same as the exalted.

The shepherds were near, yet they still needed Him. The wise men were far away, but they needed Him as well. Where do you find yourself? Are you a lost sheep having wandered afar? He's near. He's here now. Like the father who runs to greet his wasteful, irreverent, prodigal son, there will never be a time when He doesn't want you. **This entire ordeal of Him leaving glory and coming to this festering place was for you.** He came to bring you back to the Father. Call Him. He will answer. In this season that is dedicated to remembering His miraculous birth, what better gift can you give to yourself and those who love you than to yield to the Master Potter and let Him shape you beautiful, whole, and holy? Are you near? You still need Him. There will never be a time, a place, or a circumstance where you don't. So let us rejoice that He is always near and never far away.

O Come Let Us Adore Him

Draw us near, Father, so close that the image of your Son may be seen in us.

Meditation

And He came and preached peace to you who were afar off and to those who were near. For through Him we both have access by one Spirit to the Father (Eph. 2:17, 18).

Reflection

Romans 2:11 says, "For God treats everyone the same" (TLB). How does God's impartiality increase your understanding of God?

How does it increase your understanding of yourself/humanity?

How can you show acceptance to others this season?

"You know what happens when a portrait that has been painted on a panel becomes obliterated through external stains. The artist does not throw away the panel, but the subject of the portrait has to come and sit for it again, and then the likeness is re-drawn on the same material. Even so it was with the All-Holy Son of God. He, the Image of the Father, came and dwelt in our midst, in order that He might renew mankind made after Himself, and seek out His lost sheep..."

-

Bishop Athanasius of Alexandria , *On the Incaration*

17

The Good Shepherd

"I am the good shepherd. The good shepherd gives His
life for the sheep" (Jn. 10:11).

T hough shepherding was considered a lowly occupation, sheep
needed shepherds. With little ability to defend themselves, without
a shepherd, sheep are at the mercy of predators. Furthermore, since
the nature of a sheep is to follow whoever moves, having a shepherd is vital for
keeping the sheep from the danger of following the wrong leader, which could result
in neglect – even death. Sheep need a shepherd's care. So here is the Shepherd's care.

The Shepherds Care

Shepherds gently led their flock.

He will feed His flock like a shepherd; He will gather
the lambs with His arm, and carry *them* in His bosom,
and gently lead those who are with young (Isa. 40:11).

They counted their sheep as they entered the sheepfold.

In the cities of the mountains, in the cities of the lowland,
in the cities of the South, in the land of Benjamin, in

the places around Jerusalem, and in the cities of Judah, the flocks shall again pass under the hands of him who counts *them,*' says the Lord (Jer. 33:13).

If one was lost, they left the others and sought the lost one.

"What man of you, having a hundred sheep, if he loses one of them, does not leave the ninety-nine in the wilderness, and go after the one which is lost until he finds it? And when he has found *it,* he lays *it* on his shoulders, rejoicing. And when he comes home, he calls together *his* friends and neighbors, saying to them, 'Rejoice with me, for I have found my sheep which was lost!' (Lk. 15:4-6).

They guarded the sheep even at night.

Now there were in the same country shepherds living out in the fields, keeping watch over their flock by night (Lk. 2:8).

Jesus is The Good Shepherd

Jesus identified with the care of the shepherd. He called Himself the Good Shepherd who has spent so much time caring for His sheep that though sheep are prone to wander, His won't because they know His voice and will follow Him only. The Good Shepherd means that He is also the One who will not leave His sheep to be ravaged by a predator but will protect His sheep with His life – and He did.

"I am the good shepherd. The good shepherd gives His life for the sheep. But a hireling, he who is not the shepherd, one who does not own the sheep, sees the wolf coming and leaves the sheep and flees; and the wolf catches the sheep and scatters them. The hireling flees because he is a hireling and does not care about the sheep.

I am the good shepherd; and I know My sheep, and am known by My own. As the Father knows Me, even so I know the Father; and I lay down My life for the sheep. And other sheep I have which are not of this fold; them also I must bring, and they will hear My voice; and there will be one flock and one shepherd

(Jn. 10:11-16).

This Christmas season as we "Deck the Halls," drink hot chocolate, and enjoy the fellowship of family and friends, remember that Jesus is the Good

Shepherd. He is seeking you. Or perhaps, you are alone this year, and you are feeling isolated and lonely; the Good Shepherd is here. He is watching over you. When a sheep strayed, the shepherd left everything to find it. Likewise, Jesus left His place in glory to find us, the sheep that had wandered away. If the shepherd found that the sheep had been bruised or dirtied in the straying, he didn't beat the sheep for being lost. Rather, he lifted the sheep and carried her back to safety – back to where she belonged. Though we have been bruised and dirtied by our straying, Jesus still carries us close to His heart, back to where we belong. To the one who once was near and to the one who is far away, Jesus came all the way to earth so that you might have a way back to where you belong - in the Shepherd's care.

18

INCREASING

> When his time of service was completed, he returned
> home. After this his wife Elizabeth became pregnant and
> for five months remained in seclusion. "The Lord has
> done this for me," she said. "In these days he has shown
> his favor and taken away my disgrace among the people."
>
> Now indeed, Elizabeth your relative has also conceived
> a son in her old age; and this is now the sixth month for
> her who was called barren. For with God nothing will be
> impossible" (Lk. 1:36-37).

There was a time when the euphemism for pregnancy was "increasing." There is always a period between conception and delivery when, though one has conceived and is increasing, the increase isn't visible. Though for a time, she was not showing, from the moment of conception, Elizabeth, Mary's relative, was increasing. Something was happening inside, though it was not visible on the outside.

They called Elizabeth barren, incapable of producing (Lk. 1:36). Oh, but they who called her barren had judged too quickly, for they could only see in the natural realm; they could not see with spiritual eyes the great honor that God had in store. Elizabeth was about to participate in God's eschatological salvation. What God had in store for Elizabeth was life rather than death, fruitfulness instead of barrenness, beauty instead of ashes, joy rather than sorrow. Elizabeth gave birth to

John the Baptist, the harbinger of the King, the forerunner of the Messiah, whose message was the King is coming! Prepare the way of the Lord (Mt. 3:3).

Elizabeth hid for five months after she conceived, but in the dark, in isolation, in the silence, even though no one else could see, Elizabeth was increasing. However, Elizabeth was increasing even before this. Elizabeth was faithful even though she suffered this disappointment, and it was in her faithfulness though disappointed, her obedience though disgraced that she increased in godliness, and thus was prepared to carry her assignment.

Understand the darkness. Like old photographs, we, too, are developed in the dark. It is in your faithfulness in the night, in isolation, in the silence, when nothing seems to be going as you would like that God's Spirit produces character in you. You may not have delivered yet, but if you stand in faith, God will increase you! He will make you more like Jesus. In the silence, in the darkness, in the standing when you really want to fall down that He will increase you. He will increase your capacity to be like Him and thus prepare you to carry your assignment!

Jesus came to give us a way to transform through adversities, to become kinder, more loving, and wiser. As we in faith look upon Him, we are being made like Him. We are increasing in our capacity to personify His message, to share His love and joy with a world in need. What greater gift could we give to others?

O Come Let Us Adore Him

Thank you, Father, that because of Jesus, even our dark places you fill with light, even our empty spaces you fill with life, and so we have hope, an eager expectation of good even though they may call us barren, through faithfulness to you, we are continually increasing.

Meditation

"That Christ may dwell in your hearts through faith; that you, being rooted and grounded in love, may be able to comprehend with all the saints what *is* the width and length and depth and height— to know the love of Christ which passes knowledge; that you may be filled with all the fullness of God" (Eph. 3:17-19).

Reflection

Being faithful to God during adversity can cause us to develop character. How does this change the way you see challenges in your life?

In what capacity, though it may not be visible to others is God strengthening/ increasing you?

What can you do to reduce someone's suffering this season?

"Upon God's faithfulness rests our whole hope of future blessedness. Only as He is faithful will His covenants stand and His promises be honoured. Only as we have complete assurance that He is faithful may we live in peace and look forward with assurance to the life to come."

-

A.W. Tozer. The Knowledge of the Holy

19

Zacharias – "Yahweh Remembers"

> So it was, that while he was serving as priest before God
> in the order of his division, according to the custom of the
> priesthood, his lot fell to burn incense when he went into
> the temple of the Lord. And the whole multitude of the
> people was praying outside at the hour of incense. Then
> an angel of the Lord appeared to him, standing on the
> right side of the altar of incense. And when Zacharias
> saw *him,* he was troubled, and fear fell upon him (Lk.
> 1:8-11).

Zacharias means "Yahweh remembers." His story is a story of hope. Zacharias, the priest, and Elizabeth, his wife, were old and childless. Apparently, they prayed for children, but the years ticked by, and none were forthcoming. Zacharias was a priest of the Abijah division. Each priestly division was assigned temple services twice a year. The priestly duties of each priest were assigned by lot. To burn incense at the altar which was located in the Holy Place before the Holy of Holies where God's presence dwelt was an honor for which many priests were never selected. This time, providentially, that privilege fell to Zacharias.

The sacred altar of incense was situated in the center of the Holy place. The aromatic spices that were burned on the altar symbolized prayers. While the community gathered outside for corporate prayer, the priest offered incense on the heated altar and, after, would prostrate himself in supplication. While Zacharias performed this sacred duty, the angel Gabriel, who stands in the presence of God, appeared and informed Zacharias that God had heard his prayer and that he and Elizabeth would have a great son who would turn many people back to God. What had seemed impossible was possible with God; what had appeared to be denied was only delayed.

It is instructive that it was while Zacharias was serving. Zacharias was offering incense that symbolized the people's prayers, even while he believed his own went unanswered. That's faithful. *This teaches us that because we haven't heard from God, it doesn't mean God hasn't heard us.*

Have you ever felt that God has forgotten you? Do you believe that your dreams will forever be unfulfilled and your potential wasted? Stay faithful. Yahweh remembers. From the promise of the Savior in Genesis 3:15 to His birth in Matthew 1:25, Yahweh remembers and He rewards those who diligently seek Him.

List the people in your sphere of influence. Pray for them.

Some of your graces would never be discovered if it were not for your trials.

-

Charles H. Spurgeon,
Morning and Evening

20

Sing

Sarah. Rebecca. Rachel. Hannah. Elizabeth. These women had something in common – they had all been called barren. All had tried and hoped and prayed, year after year, and still could not produce. In biblical times, barrenness was disgraceful. It was presumed that God had closed the womb, which meant that the barren woman was excluded from bearing the Messiah. So, to all the natural heartache of barrenness, add *that* stigma. However, before we become forlorn, here is another list of names.

Isaac. Jacob. Joseph. Samuel. John the Baptist. Who are they? These are the sons birthed by the "barren" women. And not just any sons, each a son of renown. Each chosen by God for greatness in His kingdom establishment. Sarah birthed Isaac, who became the patriarch of God's chosen people, Israel. Rebecca birthed Jacob, whose name was changed to Israel, and who was Isaac's successor in the founding of the nation. Rachel birthed Joseph, a brilliant strategist who kept nations from starvation during 7 years of famine and became second in command in Egypt, the most influential kingdom on earth in those days. Hannah birthed Samuel, who became a priest and prophet who spoke to kings, led Israel in revival, and was so full of God that none of his prophecies ever failed" (1 Samuel 3:19). And Elizabeth birthed John the Baptist, who, as the forerunner of Jesus, led many hearts back to God and prepared Israel for the coming of their King.

So, why the drama? Why did God allow the women to suffer the pain of barrenness? I believe that God used their "barrenness" to teach this Kingdom truth: *when you learn that you are incapable of producing, when you have tried and failed over and over, when you have faced your own limitations and impotence, when you have clawed and scraped and still can't find your way through, that's when you give up on your own strength and learn to lean on the Almighty God, and God can accomplish through you far more than you could ever produce on your own.*

"Sing, O barren one, who did not bear;
break forth into singing and cry aloud,
you who have not been in labor!
For the children of the desolate one will be more
than the children of her who is married," says the LORD.
"Enlarge the place of your tent,
and let the curtains of your habitations be stretched out;
do not hold back; lengthen your cords
and strengthen your stakes.
For you will spread abroad to the right and to the left,
and your offspring will possess the nations
and will people the desolate cities (Is. 54:1-3 ESV).

Isaiah 54:1 instructs the barren to sing and shout! Shouting and singing are the sounds of fruitfulness and victory. Weeping and moaning are more in line with barrenness, so why was the barren one told to emit joyful sounds rather than sorrowful ones? Yes, it was because God promised that the barren one would produce – but it was not only that! Here's the real miracle: the barren one would be fruitful - *independent of their own labor!*

"Sing, O barren one, who did not bear;
break forth into singing and cry aloud,
you who have not been in labor!
For the children of the desolate one will be more
than the children of her who is married," says the LORD. (I added the emphasis).

Do you see that? The barren one who never pushed in labor would have more children than the one who had a husband! Why? Because God would produce for her if she relied upon Him!

Don't misunderstand, we are partners with God, soldiers in His army; we work; we plant and sow, but God gives the increase. When you rely on God rather than upon yourselves, the results will be not what you can produce, but what God can produce through you! Sing, O barren!

> "Enlarge the place of your tent,
> and let the curtains of your habitations be stretched out;
> do not hold back; lengthen your cords
> and strengthen your stakes.
> For you will spread abroad to the right and to the left,
> and your offspring will possess the nations and will people the
> desolate cities (Is. 54:2-3).

Notice in verse 2 that the barren one is told to enlarge her dwelling place. A thing is enlarged to prepare it for increase. The barren one was told to enlarge because God's efforts would bring about a God-sized increase. Her current place, current expectations, and current dreams were based upon what she could do. Now she needed to prepare for what God could do! When we are incapable and yet something beautiful is produced it is apparent that God is at work, and God receives the glory.

Do you believe that it's too late? Do you think you're too old, too young, not smart enough, ineffective, incapable? Look at all the women in Scripture who couldn't but trusted in the God who could and lean on His power to produce through you. Base your dreams and expectations not on what you can do, but on what He can do through you when you trust in Him!

But wait! There's more! Isaiah 54 is also a picture of salvation! The barren one who carries life despite the death that is in her womb foreshadows our salvation through the power of God alone. We now carry life despite the death that was in us because Jesus came to do for us what we could not do for ourselves. As our Representative He lived the perfect life that we could not live. As our Substitution, He paid the penalty for our sins upon the cross. We were barren, incapable of delivering the perfection that God's holiness required for salvation. So, Jesus lived it for us. It was His blood. His life. His labor. Our forgiveness. Our redemption. Our salvation.

You. Better. Sing.

21

For Unto Us A Child Is Born

For unto us a Child is born,
Unto us a Son is given;
And the government will be upon His shoulder.
And His name will be called
Wonderful, Counselor, Mighty God,
Everlasting Father, Prince of Peace.
Of the increase of *His* government and peace
There will be no end,
Upon the throne of David and over His kingdom,
To order it and establish it with judgment and justice
From that time forward, even forever.
The zeal of the LORD of hosts will perform this (Is. 9:6-7).

For unto us a Child is born. "For" is explanatory. An answer or explanation follows it. So here, "for" explains how a miserable, oppressed people, living in darkness and in the shadow of death, could go from gloom to gladness.

In that glorious day of peace there will no longer be the issuing of battle gear; no more the bloodstained uniforms of war; all such will be burned.

For unto us a child is born; unto us a son is given; and the government shall be upon his shoulder. These will be his royal titles: "Wonderful," "Counselor," "The Mighty God," "The Everlasting Father," "The Prince of Peace" (Is. 9:5-6 NLT).

What would take the people from blood-stained and battle-weary combatants to peace? A new government. A Child would be born, a Son would be given, and He would take their government upon His shoulders.

Now, a new governor is not necessarily a reason for rejoicing. It can be disastrous if the governor is wicked, weak, or half-witted. But if instead of being wicked, what if the governor is good, so good that we call His name Wonderful. What if, rather than being half-witted, He is wise? So wise that we call Him Counselor? What if instead of being weak, He is powerful, so powerful He is called the Mighty God? And what if to complete His credentials, He is known as the Everlasting Father and the Prince of Peace? What if *He* took up the reigns of your land? What if He were your governor, your ruler? Then Justice would roll down like waters and righteousness like a mighty stream (Amos 5:24).

"And the government shall be upon His shoulder." He came to be our governor, the executive head of state under whose structure and rule we place our lives. And we need not have anxiety because His government is a government of peace. Under the reign of the Wonderful Counselor, the Mighty God, the Everlasting Father, and the Prince of Peace His rule, we are loved and accepted into wholeness, guided and directed into purpose, and shaped and sharpened into His image. Our responsibility as citizens? To follow where He leads and to love in return - God, with all our heart, soul, and mind, that the greatest thing we can do, and then love others as we love ourselves (Mt. 22:37-39). For the law of His Kingdom is love, and He was the first to demonstrate it by His entrance (the King took the form of a slave, Php. 2:7), and His exit on the cross where He died in our place.

He came to spread His love, grace, forgiveness, and righteousness and to bring us into His Kingdom of peace. We who have been recipients of His goodwill are now His ambassadors. If we love as He loved, we will have no hate; we will do no harm, and His Kingdom of peace will spread throughout the land.

Blanket your family, friends, neighbors, and the stranger on the corner with His love that others might place themselves under the care of the One who is our "for", the answer to all our questions, the solution to our challenges. "For unto us a Child is born; Unto us a Son is given.

O Come Let Us Adore Him

Thank you, Father, that I am a citizen in Your Kingdom, ruled by Jesus the Prince of Peace. Help me uphold my duty as a citizen to love You as You should be loved and to love others as I love myself.

Meditation

Jesus said to him, "'You shall love the LORD your God with all your heart, with all your soul, and with all your mind.' This is *the* first and great commandment. And *the* second *is* like it: 'You shall love your neighbor as yourself' (Mt. 22:37-39).

Reflection

As a citizen of God's Kingdom, have you pledged your allegiance to uphold the law of His Kingdom?

In what ways can you grow in Your love for God?

In what ways can you show others the love of God this season?

What are you thankful for this season?

In the beginning was the
Word, and the Word was
with God, and the Word
was God. He was with
God in the beginning.
Through him all things
were made; without
him nothing was made
that has been made. In
him was life, and that
life was the light of all
mankind. The light
shines in the darkness,
and the darkness has not
overcome it.

The Word became flesh
and made his dwelling
among us. We have seen
his glory, the glory of the
one and only Son, who
came from the Father, full
of grace and truth.

John 1:1-5, 14 NIV

22

Can Anything Good Come Out of Nazareth

He was in the world, and the world was made through
Him, and the world did not know Him. He came to
His own, and His own did not receive Him. But as many
as received Him, to them He gave the right to become
children of God, to those who believe in His name: who
were born, not of blood, nor of the will of the flesh, nor of
the will of man, but of God (Jn. 1:10-13).

The Creator came to the world He created and was rejected. Born in Bethlehem, Jesus was raised in Nazareth of Galilee. Nazareth was so poorly perceived that even after John the Baptist identified Jesus as the Lamb of God who takes away the sin of the world, and after Peter and John identified Jesus as the One of whom Moses spoke, Nathanael, skeptical still asked, "Can anything good come out of Nazareth?" (John 1:46).

Nazareth of Galilee was in the north: Jerusalem, "the City of David" was in the south. It was presumed that Galileans were morally lax because northern Galilee was closer to pagan cities and farther away from the temple and the religious leaders in the southern, Holy City of Jerusalem in Judea. Furthermore, Samaria lay between Nazareth and Jerusalem. Samaria was a large, ethnically mixed region, and because of its racial makeup, many Jews refused to travel through it, further hindering fellowship between the northern Galileans and their southern Judean brothers. This lack of communion between brothers bred prejudices, stereotypes, and hostilities.

Thus, Galileans who spoke with an accent, were perceived as different, foreign, and were often victims of southern jokes (France 6).

> ... it means that even an impeccably Jewish Galilean in first-century Jerusalem was not among his own people; he was as much a foreigner as an Irishman in London or a Texan in New York. His accent would immediately mark him out as "not one of us," and all the communal prejudice of the supposedly superior culture of the capital city would stand against his claim to be heard even as a prophet, let alone as the "Messiah," a title which, as everyone knew, belonged to Judea" (France 6).

And yet, He came. And yet, He preached the Kingdom message of forgiveness and reconciliation.

Oh yes, something good came out of Nazareth.

23

The Book of Life

The book of the genealogy of Jesus Christ, the Son of
David, the Son of Abraham: Abraham begot Isaac, Isaac
begot Jacob, and Jacob begot Judah and his brothers
(Mt.1:1-2).

And Jacob begot Joseph the husband of Mary, of whom
was born Jesus who is called Christ (Mt.1:16).

C arolers sing outside. Lights twinkle in the windows. Cars line up to
view live Nativity scenes set up on church lawns. 'Tis the season
we celebrate life, the giving of God's Son, the birth of the world's
Savior. *Boring genealogies might seem incongruent to this bright celebration. Still,
if you know what to look for, genealogies can be exhilarating - because genealogies
reveal to whom one belongs.* Though our names are not recorded in the above
genealogy, if you have accepted the gift of God's salvation - this genealogy *is* about
you for it reveals to whom you belong. Let me show you.

Jesus is identified as the Son of Abraham. God promised Abraham that He
would bless all nations through him. Abraham believed. God considered Abraham's
faith as righteousness; thus, as the first to have his faith counted as righteousness,
Abraham became the father of all of us who are saved by faith.

God's promise to bless all nations would come through Abraham's
offspring. Sarah, Abraham's wife, at 90 years old had a miracle child, Isaac. But
Isaac wasn't that offspring. Isaac had Jacob. But Jacob wasn't that offspring. No,

because the promise of God to bless all nations through Abraham was spoken not of all Abraham's offspring *but to one particular offspring - Jesus.* Jesus, the Son of God, the Savior of the world, came through Abraham's descendants; thus He is called the Son of Abraham, and thus the Father fulfilled His promise to bless all nations through Abraham's lineage. Through faith in Jesus, all nations have been given the right to become sons and daughters of God - heirs of eternal salvation. Now that's a blessing.

Therefore, with the birth of Jesus, the Son of Abraham, this genealogy becomes more than just a lineage of Abraham's *natural* offspring, this genealogy also anticipates the birth of those who would believe in Jesus and become sons and daughters by faith. So, if this genealogy had been extended to include Abraham's *spiritual offspring, then my name would have been added, and your name, too, if you have been saved by your faith in Jesus.*

If the record could have been extended to include Abraham's spiritual offspring, it would have contained the other children of God, the ones who were adopted into the family, grafted into the vine, and bought by the Blood of the Lamb. *If you want those names, they are not here, but they are recorded in another book, the Lamb's Book of Life.* The Book of Life is a record of all those who have passed from death to eternal life through the blood of the Lamb, the Son of Abraham, the virgin-born Son of God whose coming has made we who believe sons and daughters of Almighty God.

O Come Let Us Adore Him

Thank you, Father, that because of Jesus, the Son of Abraham, the Son of God, my name is written in the Lamb's Book of Life.

Meditation

Everyone who conquers will be clothed in white, and I will not erase his name from the Book of Life, but I will announce before my Father and his angels that he is mine (Rev. 3:5 TLB).

Reflection

Reflect upon what it means to have life everlasting because of what the Savior did.

How will gratitude for His sacrifice change how you celebrate this season?

24

Worship

> And when they were come into the house, they saw the young child with Mary his mother, and fell down, and worshipped him: and when they had opened their treasures, they presented unto him gifts; gold, and frankincense and myrrh (Mt. 2:11).

A round the throne of the Almighty that flashes with lightning, rumblings, and thunder, four living creatures worship day and night, saying, "Holy, holy, holy is the Lord God Almighty" (Rev 4:8, ESV). The four living creatures are full of eyes, full of insight (no wonder they never cease to worship). When the four living creatures worship, twenty-four elders wearing golden crowns fall prostrate before the Almighty and cast their crowns at His feet, saying,

> "You are worthy, O Lord,
> To receive glory and honor and power;
> For You created all things,
> And by Your will they exist and were created" (Rev. 4:11).

Remarkable. When the elders throw what represents authority, victory, and accomplishment at the feet of the Almighty, their message is unmistakable. God alone is worthy. He is the only Sovereign, the One whose character and power give Him the right to rule. Whatever good, whatever accomplishments that have been credited to them, to any of us, really belong to the One in Whom we live and breathe and have our being. *When we, like the four living creatures, are full of eyes to see and insight to understand, we too will discern that the only proper response to the splendor of God is a life of worship.*

Worship is "worth" ship, recognizing His worth. He is the Wonderful Counselor, the Lion of the tribe of Judah, the Way the Truth and the Life, the door unto the Father, purchaser of our salvation, the sinless, holy, Son of Almighty God, God in human form, then the only proper response is to fall down before him as did the wise men and worship.

The wise men searched for Him. Beckoned by a star, they had kissed their loved ones goodbye, traversed miles of challenging terrain, and braved uncaring elements to find Him, and when they found He for whom they searched, the King of kings, the divine within human flesh, they fell prostrate before Him.

As an outward showing of their inner conviction, they gave to Him King-worthy gifts, gold, frankincense, and myrrh. They understood that to stoop but not to sacrifice, to genuflect but not to give your best is not worship. To bow, to prostrate oneself is easy. Demons did it. To worship is more than bending the knee, but a bowing of the heart in reverence, and when one has worshipped, it means withholding nothing.

We are God's treasures. Within us, He has placed His most valuable gift, His Spirit, Who has given us the gifts of God as He has seen fit (1 Cor. 12:4-11). Ironically, when we worship God and render to Him what He is due, withhold nothing, we are merely returning to Him what He has given us.

Do you recognize His worth?

O Come Let Us Adore Him

Meditation

"But the hour is coming, and is now here, when the true worshipers will worship the Father in spirit and truth, for the Father is seeking such people to worship him. God is spirit, and those who worship him must worship in spirit and truth" (Jn. 4:23,24).

Reflection

The wise men devoted time to seeking Jesus and offering homage. In what ways can you prioritize worship in your life?

25

Pageantry

For there is born to you this day in the city of David a
Savior, who is Christ the Lord (Lk. 2:11).

I saw a parade on television. You know the big, magnificent parade that
happens each Thanksgiving Day? It was full of gigantic floats, music,
marching bands, and world-class singers. The crowd, snuggled in their
winter gear, cheered and danced. Little ones squealing and waving pom poms sat
on their father's shoulders as balloons shaped like cartoon characters and animals
floated by.

The gaiety and pageantry were infectious. Right at the end of this over-one-
hour extravaganza, a television network host joyfully announced that "the star of
our holiday season" would soon make his entrance. With the crowd cheering and a
marching band playing "Santa Claus is Coming to Town," in rolled Santa Claus on
a giant float outfitted with a large sleigh and 8 full-scale prop reindeer appearing on
the cusp of flight from a snow-covered roof of a prop house. Elves and Mrs. Clause
waved and smiled while Santa stood from his sleigh and cheered. Floating in the air
near Santa were balloons with the word, "Believe."

This is the Christmas season, the "Christ Mass," and in this multi-million-
dollar celebration, I heard no mention of the actual "star of the season," the One who
was born in the city of David, our Savior Christ the Lord. *Ironic. Christ was born*

without pageantry, and now in the season we dedicate to His celebration, we have pageantry – but without Him.

It would be tragic to celebrate Christmas and reject Christ, to supplant the Savior with Santa Claus, to see a babe in a manger and miss the God in human flesh. It is tragic because to miss the truth for the trappings is missing out on who He was, what He gave, and why He came.

God came for us. When we could not cross the sin chasm that separated us from the goodness of God, Jesus became the bridge. When we could not lift ourselves up to reach God, God lowered Himself and came down to us. He came to stand in our place, endure our penalty, to reconnect us to Himself, to bring us into His Kingdom of justice, to show us how to walk in love toward God and our fellow man, to bring peace, so we may rejoice with exceedingly great joy. All of this we gain if we will do as the balloon that waved around the mythical Santa's sleigh stated – if we, "Believe." Believe in Jesus and His work on the Cross. Santa is said to bring gifts. Jesus gives purpose in this life and everlasting life in the age to come. The truth is superior to the trappings.

Let us remember the true "star of the holiday season," and let us, like the wise men, see His brightness, behold His glory and prostrate before Him. And let us - all of us who have been utterly altered by His presence join with the chorus of those who call Him Immanuel and celebrate that we were so valuable that one day, wrapped in swaddling cloths and clothed in flesh, God came to save us from our sins.

O Come Let Us Adore Him

Meditation

"Oh come, let us sing to the Lord! Let us shout joyfully to the Rock of our salvation. Let us come before His presence with thanksgiving; let us shout joyfully to Him with psalms. For the Lord is the great God, and the great King above all gods" (Ps. 95:1-3).

Reflection

What does the Incarnation Christ mean to you?

What are you thankful for?

How will you share it with others?

Thank you for reading!
The author would love the honor of your review.

Works Cited

France, R. T., The Gospel of Matthew (The New International Commentary on the New Testament) (p. 6). Wm. B. Eerdmans Publishing Co.. Kindle Edition.

Garland, David E., Clinton E. Arnold. Luke (Zondervan Exegetical Commentary on the New Testament) (Kindle Location 2636). Zondervan. Kindle Edition.

Green, Joel B., The Gospel of Luke. Wm. B. Eerdmans Publishing Co.. Kindle Edition, 1997.

Hrynowski, Z. (2019). *More Americans Celebrating a Secular Christmas*. Gallup. news.gallup.com.

Made in the USA
Las Vegas, NV
28 November 2022